COUNTRIES OF THE WORLD

KENYA

ROB BOWDEN

Evans

TITLES IN THE COUNTRIES OF THE WORLD SERIES:
BRAZIL • FRANCE • JAPAN • KENYA • UNITED KINGDOM • USA

Published by Evans Brothers Limited
2A Portman Mansions
Chiltern Street
London W1U 6NR

Produced for Evans Brothers Limited by
Monkey Puzzle Media Limited
Gissing's Farm, Fressingfield
Suffolk IP21 5SH

First published 2002
© copyright Evans Brothers 2002
© copyright in the text Rob Bowden 2002
© copyright in the photographs Rob Bowden 2002

British Library Cataloguing in Publication Data
Kenya. - (Countries of the world)
1.Kenya - Juvenile literature
I.Title
967.6'2

ISBN 0 237 52269 1

Editor: Katie Orchard
Designer: Jane Hawkins
Photographs by Rob Bowden (images@easi-er.co.uk)
Map artwork by Peter Bull
Charts and graphs produced by Alex Pang

Endpapers (front): Stunning fertile farmland in the
western highlands of Kenya.
Title page: Subsistence farmers sell their produce on
a small stall.
Imprint and Contents page: Kericho tea plantation
stretches as far as the eye can see.
Endpapers (back): An aerial view of central Nairobi.

CONTENTS

The Kenyan flag, introduced in 1963 after independence.
The Masai warrior's shield in the centre represents the
defence of freedom.

INTRODUCING KENYA

Kenya is famed for wildlife such as these elegant topi in the Masai Mara.

AN AMBASSADOR FOR AFRICA

Kenya accounts for less than 2 per cent of Africa's total area, yet to many it symbolises everything African. The teeming wildlife of the Masai Mara, the spectacular landscapes of the Great Rift Valley and the striking beauty of Kenya's people have become familiar images the world over, attracting hundreds of thousands of visitors every year. Novels and films such as *Out of Africa* and *Born Free* have further popularised Kenya, and made it a true ambassador for the African continent.

But there is another side to Kenya that is not so widely portrayed. For millions of Kenyans, the natural wonders of their surroundings are merely a backdrop to their struggle for progress and development. Kenya remains one of the poorest countries in the world with over half the population living on less than US$1 per day. Life expectancy is just 51 years compared to 77 in the UK and USA and 10 per cent of Kenya's children will die before their fifth birthday.

Up to 40 per cent of the population are unable to complete their primary schooling and around 20 per cent of adults are illiterate. Even basic provisions, such as safe drinking water are missing for over half the population.

A COUNTRY OF CONTRASTS

These two very different sides of Kenya are typical of the country as a whole. It is a diverse land, with extreme contrasts to be found in all aspects of life. History has played an important role in shaping contemporary Kenya, particularly the period of British colonial rule, which ended in 1963. But Arabic influences stretch back even further, to the early days of trading and slavery. Today, Kenya has links with countries throughout the world and is a leader in East Africa. The capital, Nairobi, has become one of the most important cities in the world. It is home to both the environmental and human settlement programmes of the United Nations (UN) and provides an African base for numerous international organisations and businesses.

With such diversity in a single country it is perhaps little wonder that Kenya attracts so much attention, but what of its future? In a country already struggling with rapid population growth and a deteriorating environment, the very values that make Kenya such a special place are under threat

Nairobi is one of the most important cities in Africa and a major business centre.

from all manner of factors. The first few decades of the twenty-first century will prove to be a testing time. Central to Kenya's success will be its ability to overcome the enormous variations in wealth that lead to tensions and mistrust among the different groups of society. The wealthiest fifth of the population earn around twenty times more than the poorest fifth, with signs that this divide is widening further. Despite these difficulties, most Kenyan people remain proud of their country and optimistic about its future.

Pokot women still wear their beautiful traditional necklaces and jewellery.

KEY DATA

Official Name:	Republic of Kenya (*Jamhuri ya Kenya*)
Area:	582,646km^2
Population:	29 million (mid-2000 estimate)
Official Languages:	Swahili and English
Main Cities:	Nairobi (capital), Mombasa, Kisumu, Eldoret, Nakuru
GDP per Capita:	US$1,022 (1999)*
Currency:	Kenyan Shilling (K Sh)
Exchange Rate:	US$1 = 78K Sh £1 = 112K Sh (mid-2001)

* Calculated on Purchasing Power Parity basis
Source: United Nations Agencies

LANDSCAPE AND CLIMATE

The Great Rift Valley, seen from the escarpment north of Nairobi.

THE GREAT RIFT VALLEY

Kenya's landscape is dominated by the Great Rift Valley, which cuts across the entire length of the country, extending north into Ethiopia and south into Tanzania. Its dramatic escarpments rise gradually from the surrounding plains to heights of well over 2,000m, before dropping 1,000m or more into the valley floor between them. The Mau Escarpment, the Aberdare Range and the Cherangani Hills are some of the highest parts of the system, at between 3,000 and 4,000m.

FORMATION OF THE VALLEY

In its entirety the rift system, more correctly known as the Afro-Arabian Rift, extends 6,500km in length and is one of a small number of the earth's natural features clearly visible from space. Its width varies considerably, but within Kenya it ranges from 40km at its narrowest to around 320km at its widest point.

The rift system visible today is the result of a series of parallel faults in the earth's crust that have slowly moved apart, causing the land in between to sink and form the valley. At the same time, volcanic activity within the valley deposited millions of tonnes of lava and ash, filling it up almost as fast as it was being formed. In parts of Kenya this layer of lava and ash is thought to be 3km deep or more. The Great Rift Valley is no longer a region of major geographical change. The last big movement was the Subukia earthquake in 1928 along the Laikipia escarpment east of Lake Bogoria. As well as the stunning views and unique lake ecosystems that attract tourists from around the world, the Great Rift Valley supplies Kenya with a variety of natural resources.

A YOUNG SYSTEM

Despite its enormous size, the rift system is actually very young in geological terms, being formed perhaps as recently as 40 million years ago. This can be put into perspective by condensing the planet's geological history into the equivalent of just an hour. Using this method, the rift valley was formed only 32 seconds ago.

The highland escarpments provide the best farmland in the country, and some of the best in Africa, even the world.

A Land of Mountains...

Just beyond the main rift system is a series of mountains formed by molten lava forcing its way up through cracks in the earth's crust as the rift valley fractured and formed. Mount Elgon straddles the western border between Kenya and Uganda and reaches 4,321m at its summit. Mount Kenya, or 'Kirinyaga' as it is locally known, lies just to the east of the Aberdares and rises to 5,199m, making it the highest point in Kenya. Despite being positioned virtually on the Equator, it is cold enough to have ice and snow fields on its summit throughout the year. Perhaps the most famous mountain of all, however, is the snow-capped dome of Kilimanjaro. At 5,895m this is the highest peak in Africa. Situated across the Tanzanian border, Kilimanjaro is clearly visible from a large area of southern Kenya and provides a spectacular backdrop to Amboseli National Park. All three mountains are popular tourist attractions, with many thousands of walkers arriving each year for the trek to reach one of the summits.

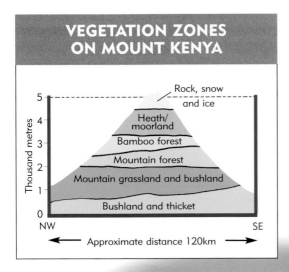

VEGETATION ZONES ON MOUNT KENYA

Rock, snow and ice

Heath/moorland

Bamboo forest

Mountain forest

Mountain grassland and bushland

Bushland and thicket

Thousand metres

NW · SE

Approximate distance 120km

MAIN PICTURE: Africa's most famous mountain, Kilimanjaro, can be seen clearly from Amboseli National Park.

INSET: Fischer's column is an old volcanic plug, which rises dramatically from the floor of Hell's Gate National Park near Naivasha.

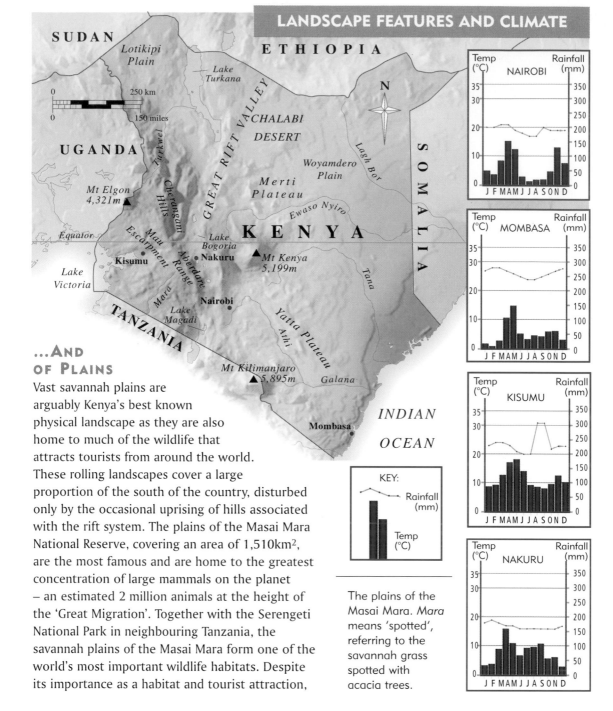

Temp (°C) / Rainfall (mm) — NAIROBI

Temp (°C) / Rainfall (mm) — MOMBASA

Temp (°C) / Rainfall (mm) — KISUMU

Temp (°C) / Rainfall (mm) — NAKURU

KEY:
—— Rainfall (mm)
▮ Temp (°C)

The plains of the Masai Mara. *Mara* means 'spotted', referring to the savannah grass spotted with acacia trees.

...AND OF PLAINS

Vast savannah plains are arguably Kenya's best known physical landscape as they are also home to much of the wildlife that attracts tourists from around the world. These rolling landscapes cover a large proportion of the south of the country, disturbed only by the occasional uprising of hills associated with the rift system. The plains of the Masai Mara National Reserve, covering an area of 1,510km², are the most famous and are home to the greatest concentration of large mammals on the planet – an estimated 2 million animals at the height of the 'Great Migration'. Together with the Serengeti National Park in neighbouring Tanzania, the savannah plains of the Masai Mara form one of the world's most important wildlife habitats. Despite its importance as a habitat and tourist attraction,

The Masai Mara is famous for the annual migration of wildebeest and zebra from the Serengeti National Park in Tanzania. Each year, beginning in June or July, up to a million and a half wildebeest and 250,000 zebra make a frenzied crossing of the Mara River, which divides the two parks (and countries). Thousands drown or perish as crocodiles and lions wait in ambush for their seasonal feast. The animals make this epic crossing as they follow the long rains north to take advantage of the freshly watered savannah grasses of the Mara. Then, before being stranded by the shorter rains towards the end of October, they head south again for their return journey to the Serengeti – a round trip of some 2,800km. A visit to the Mara in August to witness this spectacle is an unforgettable experience.

Heavily eroded banks of the Mara River show one of the crossing points for the Great Migration.

the Masai Mara is small compared to the enormous savannah plains of Tsavo National Park. Spanning an area of 20,810km² Tsavo is the largest park in Kenya and the fifth-largest in Africa. However, the greatest area of plains, covering around two-thirds of the country, are the arid lands of north and north-east Kenya. These are dominated by desert or desert scrub and are sparsely populated with nomadic pastoralists pursuing what little vegetation and water there is to sustain their livestock.

A VARIED CLIMATE

Kenya's climate is as varied as its landscape, but could be summarised as generally warm and dry. Its location on the Equator means that temperatures change very little over the year. In fact there is a greater variation between day and night-time temperatures (diurnal temperature range) than there is across the year (annual temperature range). This is a characteristic of countries that lie between the tropics of Cancer (23.5°N) and Capricorn (23.5°S). Despite the relative stability of temperatures, averages vary dramatically across the country, mainly due to altitude. The low coastal and inland plains (0–1,000m) experience temperatures of 28°C, with 35°C or higher not uncommon inland from the cooling ocean breezes. The highlands to the north and west of Nairobi by contrast are much cooler, with temperatures falling by about 0.6°C for every 100m increase in altitude – known as the lapse rate. Above 4,000m, average temperatures rarely exceed 10–12°C and fall to near freezing point towards the summit of Mount Kenya.

Rainfall in Kenya is generally low in all areas apart from the highlands, the coastal strip and the basin of Lake Victoria. Much of Kenya can be classified as semi-arid or arid, receiving less than 500mm of rainfall per year. The rains normally arrive in two seasons; the long rains between March and May and the short rains between late October and December.

Villagers take shelter from a sudden downpour at the start of Kenya's long rains.

WHEN THE RAINS COME

The rains bring a flurry of activity for the 80 per cent of Kenyans involved in agriculture as they prepare land and plant crops to take advantage of the seasonal weather. For many others, however, the rainy seasons can bring hardships. It is the low season for tourists, and diseases associated with water, such as malaria, cholera and typhoid, become more common. More significant than seasonality, however, is the unreliability of rainfall. In 2000, the short rains failed across much of the country, following long rains that were not only late, but at least 25 per cent below their normal levels. This led to low or failed harvests and widespread livestock deaths, particularly in northern areas of the country. In other years parts of Kenya have received too much rainfall, causing damage to large sections of road and railway, and flooding fields and villages. Such variation in the timing, volume and intensity of rainfall makes crop cultivation extremely risky for farmers and presents a major problem for Kenya's food supply.

THE COAST

Kenya benefits from 536km of stunning coastline, bordering the Indian Ocean. Endless stretches of white sand are fringed by coconut palms and mangrove swamps, whilst the warm tropical

CASE STUDY
DROUGHT

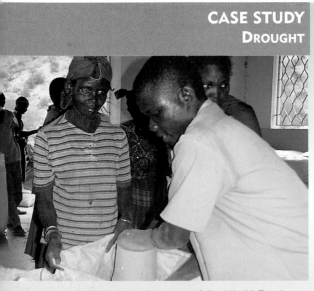

Maize is distributed as part of the World Food Programme's drought relief programme in 2001.

In February 2001, the United Nations World Food Programme (WFP) appealed for food to feed 4.4 million Kenyans as part of its ongoing drought relief operation. In 2000, Kenya's short rains were late and failed to alleviate the effects of drought that had been present for four growing seasons in some districts. Successive droughts make it hard for people to survive, let alone recover. Many of those most affected were pastoral communities in northern districts who depend almost entirely on livestock. After a prolonged period of drought it can take many years to restock herds. The WFP stated that in 2000 Kenya's emergency food operation was the third-largest in the world. In 2001, 86 per cent of the country was included in relief operations. Drought may become more frequent in the future due to a growing population and drier climatic conditions.

waters sustain coral reefs, rivalled only by those of the Great Barrier Reef and the Red Sea. This rich coastal strip is a tourist paradise, with over 60 per cent of all visitors spending part of their holiday in the resorts to the north and south of Mombasa. The coastal strip has a hot and humid climate. Mombasa's old town was even designed with the climate in mind, with tall buildings and narrow streets providing cool shade on even the hottest of days.

LAKE VICTORIA

The only other place in Kenya with such a hot and humid climate is the south-west corner around Lake Victoria. Despite its location, Lake Victoria is not part of the rift valley system, although it is fed by several rivers such as the Mara that rise in the rift valley. Lake Victoria generates regular rainfall over Kenya's western highlands – the agricultural heartland of Kenya and the centre of the tea industry. Without Lake Victoria, this area would be a lot drier and much of the agriculture currently practised in the region would not be possible.

The palm-fringed beaches of the Indian Ocean make Kenya's coast a major tourist destination.

EFFECTS OF EL NIÑO

In 1997–98 Kenya experienced extreme rainfall associated with the El Niño events of that year. Parts of the country received 'dry season' rainfall 50 times greater than that normally expected leading to crop failures, livestock deaths, transport disruption and disease outbreaks.

Rain clouds gather over Lake Victoria.

NATURAL RESOURCES

Lake Turkana

● National Parks

● National Reserve

Sibiloi

Malka Mari

Central Island

Turkwel

South Island

Marsabit

Lagh Bor

Nasolot

South Turkana

Saiwa Swamp

Maralal

Ewaso Nyiro

Mt Elgon

Samburu

Shaba

Kakamega

Buffalo Springs

Lake Bogoria

Meru

Bisanadi

Rahole

Equator

Lake Nakuru

Mt Kenya

Kora

Ruma

Aberdare

Mwingi

Tana

Mara

Hell's Gate

Arawale

Masai Mara

Lake Magadi

Nairobi

South Kitui

Boni

Dodori

Kimana Nature Reserve

Kiunga Marine Reserve

Amboseli

Chyulu Hills

Tsavo East

Tsavo West

Malindi/Watamu Marine Parks and Reserves

Shimba Hills

Mombasa Marine Park and Reserve

Diani/Chale

At first glance, Kenya appears to be a country lacking in natural resources: it has no large deposits of gold, diamonds or oil, for example. It does, however, have some of the best flora and fauna the world can offer, set within stunning physical landscapes. Such resources are often overlooked, but they are essential to the tourist industry, which for many years has been one of Kenya's primary sources of income.

Take away the tropical beaches, the teeming savannah plains and the thriving lakes and few tourists would come to Kenya. Yet, as with many resources, Kenya's natural wonders are under increasing pressure from human actions.

In 1970, Kenya had a population of some 170,000 elephants, but by the early 1990s poaching and habitat destruction had reduced this figure to just 20,000. White rhino populations suffered an even more dramatic collapse from 20,000 to only 300 for the same

reasons, over a similar time period. In total, some 200 species in Kenya are classified as endangered by the IUCN (International Union for the Conservation of Nature), though in reality the figure is probably higher. Habitats are also under increasing pressure. Forests are felled for their timber, for fuel, or for use as farmland, affecting water catchments and increasing soil erosion. Wetlands are also reclaimed for agriculture or are simply drying out as the water feeding them is used further upstream.

Kakamega Forest is the last remnant of tropical rainforest in Kenya. But it remains under extreme pressure from local communities.

Industrial and agricultural pollution contaminates watercourses and soils, mangrove swamps are cleared to make way for tourist resorts, and coral reefs suffer marine pollution, over-fishing and mining to make tourist souvenirs.

NATURE: PROBLEM OR RESOURCE?

Central to this species and environment loss is Kenya's struggle to appreciate nature as a resource. In Kenya, nature is often considered a barrier to the country's development. The Masai, for example, consider the land that makes up the Masai Mara Reserve and Amboseli National Park to be rightfully theirs and the wildlife as unwanted invaders of their land. For the Masai, the enormous herds of wildebeest are 'wild cattle', competing with

their livestock for pasture and water, and bringing diseases to their herds. Elsewhere, large cats, such as lions, leopards and cheetahs are considered pests for killing livestock, and elephants are despised for the damage they cause to property and crops.

Thankfully, nature is now being recognised as one of Kenya's greatest resources. The national parks and reserves now work more closely with local groups to explore ways in which people and wildlife can all benefit. This new approach is spreading throughout Kenya and numbers, for some species at least, are beginning to increase again.

PARKS v PEOPLE?

Only 7.5 per cent of Kenya's land is set aside as protected areas such as parks or reserves, whilst more than 80 per cent of Kenya's biodiversity is found outside these areas. With rapid population growth in Kenya, people and wildlife are coming into greater conflict as competition for land increases. Landowners determine how such land is used and as they are usually interested in earning money from it, wildlife and natural vegetation are normally considered a nuisance.

The elephant population is increasing again, thanks to conservation and anti-poaching policies.

CASE STUDY
KIMANA COMMUNITY WILDLIFE SANCTUARY

Sanctuaries such as Kimana provide protection for animals such as giraffes that roam far beyond park boundaries.

Just east of Amboseli National Park lies Kimana Community Wildlife Sanctuary, a flagship eco-tourism project that is leading the way to people recognising wildlife and natural habitats as valuable natural resources. Started in 1994, the sanctuary covers 40km^2 of a Masai ranch and is home to a wealth of wildlife, including four of the 'big five' (lion, leopard, elephant, buffalo and rhino) – but there are no rhinos in Kimana. Kimana is the first wildlife scheme in Kenya to be fully owned and operated by a local community. Profits are divided amongst the local Masai, with a proportion being re-invested into local development projects. Realising the rewards of their natural surroundings, the Masai of Kimana now actively protect this resource. Some even consider it a more reliable source of income than their livestock. In 1996, Kimana won a prize for the best international tourism project of the year. Similar projects, inspired by the success of Kimana, are now opening up throughout Kenya, suggesting a brighter future for both wildlife and the communities who share their lives with it.

NATIONAL PARKS

Nairobi National Park was the first national park to be established in Kenya, in 1946. Since then, a further 58 national parks, reserves or protected areas have been established across the country.

A RICH RESOURCE

The land surrounding Lake Victoria is one of the most densely populated areas of the country. Lake Victoria is a vast body of water, covering a total of 68,000km^2 – an area almost the size of Ireland – and rich in natural resources. Kenya controls just 6 per cent (4,100km^2) of Lake Victoria, but the lake is intensively used. Almost 85 per cent of Kenya's fish comes from the lake, supporting an estimated 35,000 fishermen and their families. People involved in cleaning, transporting and trading fish are also dependent on the lake for their livelihoods.

FISHERIES BOOM...

Fishing has supported the local people around Lake Victoria for hundreds of years. During the 1980s the fish catch boomed from 100,000 tonnes in 1979 to 500,000 tonnes by 1990. This was triggered by the introduction of Nile perch to the lake in 1954 and later, a fish called tilapia. Both species bred rapidly (especially the Nile perch) and today, along with a sardine-like fish called omena, they make up almost the total fish catch. Big businesses became interested in the fisheries when they realised the potential of Lake Victoria as a major natural resource. Today, Kenyan fish (mainly Nile perch and tilapia) are processed and exported to supermarkets as far away as Europe, Israel and Australia. This trade earns valuable foreign income for the Kenyan economy as well as supporting thousands of jobs.

...AND BUST

Unfortunately, changes in the use of Lake Victoria have also created some problems. A large proportion of local fish species have become extinct following the introduction of Nile perch and tilapia. These local species (haplochromis) once made up over 80 per cent of the fish in Lake Victoria and performed important ecological functions, such as recycling oxygen and nutrients to keep the water healthy. Today, haplochromis make up less than 1 per cent of the fish and the lake ecosystem is less healthy as a result. Over-fishing is also placing extreme pressure on the lake's resources. Fish are caught before they have had the opportunity to breed successfully, leading to the double problem of smaller and fewer fish being caught. A full-grown Nile perch can weigh as much as 200kg, but fish processors now regularly

Over-fishing means that the Nile perch caught today are much smaller than they used to be.

accept fish weighing as little as 0.8kg. Regulations such as limits on the size of net mesh used have been introduced to control fishing, but they are proving very difficult to monitor. As a result, Lake Victoria's fisheries remain under pressure and their long-term future is in serious doubt.

Traders and buyers bargain with fishermen over the morning catch at Dunga beach, near Kisumu.

FERTILE SOILS

Kenya has some of the best farmland in the world, thanks to a combination of fertile volcanic soils and near-perfect climatic conditions for growth. Much of the most productive farmland was occupied by British farmers during the colonial period and used to grow products for export back to Britain. This historical influence can be seen today, with most of the best land still used to grow tea and coffee – two of Kenya's most important products for export. Sugar, rice and maize are among the other crops grown commercially in the highlands. More recently, horticulture (the growing of vegetables and flowers) has become big business, with hundreds of farms taking advantage of the growing conditions to produce high-quality, high-value export crops. There is little doubt that Kenya's fertile soils are among its greatest natural resources, producing some of its most valuable products. But there are those who criticise the use of the most productive land for growing export crops instead of meeting the local demand for food. They point out the irony of Kenya being among the world's biggest producers of tea, coffee and flowers (all non-edible products) whilst becoming increasingly dependent on

Limestone, used to manufacture cement, is mined at several sites in Kenya.

imported food grains (mainly maize) to prevent starvation, which threatened 4 million people in 2001.

MINERALS

Kenya's mineral wealth is limited to a few isolated regions and to specific deposits of certain minerals. Limestone, used to make cement, is found in various locations, but the Bamburi cement works near Mombasa is perhaps the best known, having been operational since 1954. With such a rapidly expanding population, much of Kenya's cement production is used internally for construction and road building, to cope with the increasing demand for housing and transport links. In 1995, Kenya consumed 1,056,000 tonnes of cement, but a lack of funds for public buildings and road

CEMENT PRODUCTION IN KENYA

Thousand tonnes

1,600
1,200
800
400
0

1970   1980   1990   1995

Source: *Geographical Digest*, 1998–99

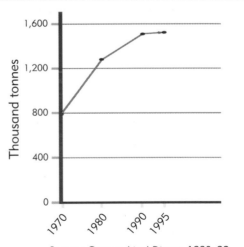

RIGHT: Gold panning is a useful source of income for this Pokot woman.

construction has caused consumption to decline by more than 25 per cent in recent years to just 769,500 tonnes by 1998.

The mineral fluorite (used for its fluorescent qualities) is found in the Kerio Valley and has been mined in increasing quantities during the 1990s. Further south, the Magadi Soda Company produces over 250,000 tonnes of soda ash per year. This is Kenya's most valuable mineral export.

Gold is present in small quantities and is collected mainly by local people (normally women) panning the silt in streams. The tiny amounts found are taken to local markets, where they are sold to gold dealers from Nairobi. Although it is only small-scale, gold panning provides an important income for women in remote rural areas such as West Pokot and Marakwet. One important mineral is soapstone, a soft stone with a beautiful grain and colour. Soapstone is mined near Kisii, but sold throughout Kenya and beyond in the form of carved tourist souvenirs such as sculptures, plates and chess sets.

BELOW: Soapstone, mined at Kisii, is used to make some of Kenya's most popular tourist souvenirs.

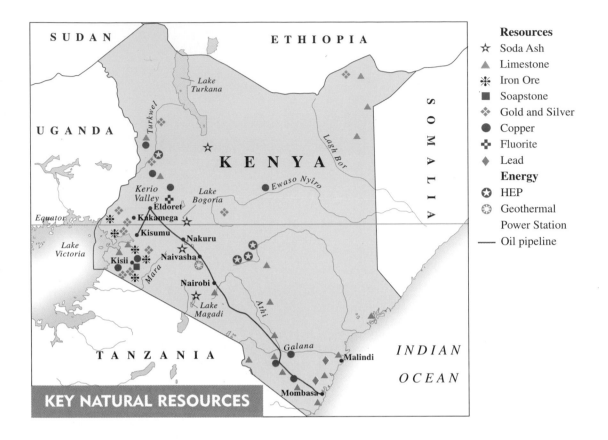

KEY NATURAL RESOURCES

Resources
- ☆ Soda Ash
- ▲ Limestone
- ❋ Iron Ore
- ■ Soapstone
- ❖ Gold and Silver
- ● Copper
- ✚ Fluorite
- ◆ Lead

Energy
- ✪ HEP
- ✺ Geothermal Power Station
- — Oil pipeline

ENERGY

With no reserves of petroleum, Kenya relies on imported oil, which is refined at Changamwe oil refinery in Mombasa.

Superheated steam rising from deep underground is trapped and piped to Olkaria geothermal power station.

Oil accounts for almost 15 per cent of Kenya's import costs, but a proportion of this is recovered by exporting refined petroleum to neighbouring countries, such as Uganda and the Democratic Republic of the Congo. In total the export of petroleum products accounts for around 5 per cent of Kenya's export earnings. Within Kenya, the refined oil is transported along a 483-km pipeline from Mombasa to the major population centres, finally ending up in Kisumu.

In the absence of fossil fuels Kenya relies on hydroelectric power (HEP) for around 80 per cent of its power generation, with most of this coming from dams constructed along the Tana River. Superheated volcanic steam from deep inside the rift valley is also used to generate electricity at Olkaria geothermal power station, near Naivasha. This currently produces around 8 per cent of Kenya's power, but this figure is expected to increase with the construction of a second power station started in 2001.

KEEPING UP WITH DEMAND

Demand for electricity has increased dramatically from just 109 kilowatt-hours per capita in 1980 to 154 kilowatt-hours per capita in 1997 – a 41 per cent increase. Regular power cuts are evidence that Kenya needs to develop its energy sector further as demand for electricity continues to grow. To meet this shortfall, Kenya has been importing electricity from neighbouring Uganda, but as demand for power in Uganda increases this will become less available. Several new HEP schemes are under construction to meet future demand. There is some doubt about the benefit of more HEP dams, however, following the disappointing performance of some recent projects. Most of Kenya's major rivers have already been dammed, and with drier conditions and lower river levels expected

Millions of people still rely on biomass fuels for energy. This woman is making charcoal.

in the future, some believe there is simply not enough water to generate a reliable supply of electricity.

CASE STUDY
TURKWEL GORGE DAM

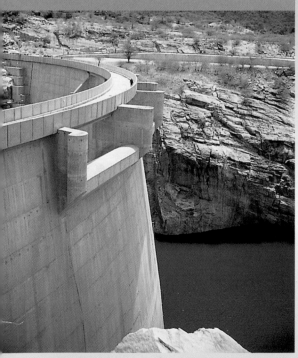

Low water levels at Turkwel Gorge Dam mean it has failed to meet its aims.

Above the arid drylands south of Lake Turkana is the Turkwel Gorge Multi-purpose Project. The main feature of the project is a large dam standing 110m high and spanning 160m in a giant arc across the Turkwel gorge. The narrow gorge is well suited for a dam and the fall of water to the valley floor below creates a strong force of water for generating electricity. At full capacity Turkwel alone would produce 15 per cent of the country's electricity, but Turkwel has yet to fulfil this potential. The level of the lake has never risen high enough for permanent power generation and some believe it never will because of the low rainfall in the region. In addition to the poor record of electricity generation, other proposed benefits such as irrigation, new fisheries, recreation facilities and water regulation have never been developed. Local people have not benefited at all from the scheme – most remain without electricity and water! Many now accuse the government of wasting money on the project and say it was only built because members of the government would profit from it – they believe this is an example of corruption.

PEOPLE OF KENYA

Nairobi is a multicultural city, influenced by all sectors of Kenya's population.

Kenya's population reflects not only its varied environment, but also the links it has built with other parts of the world throughout its history. The majority of the population are black Africans, but the small minority of Asians, Arabs and Europeans that make up around 1 per cent of the population are very significant to the economy – owning or controlling many of Kenya's most valuable businesses. The presence of these minority populations is tied closely to Kenya's history.

EARLY TRADING

Arabic people first arrived in Kenya as traders, setting up coastal settlements over 1,000 years ago. The coastal towns of Mombasa, Malindi and Lamu were all former trading posts, and evidence of Arabic architecture and culture is still strong there.

In 1498 Vasco da Gama, a Portuguese explorer, was the first European to reach the east coast of Africa. Within four years, the Portuguese had established trading settlements in what is now Malindi. However, they soon relocated to Mombasa, where they constructed Fort Jesus to protect the natural harbour from invaders. Completed in 1593, Fort Jesus has played a key role in the coast's history, including the great siege of the fort by Oman Arabs (13 March 1696 – 13 December 1698), which ended with the expulsion of the Portuguese from the Kenyan coast and led to another period of Arab control. Today, some 40,000 people of Arabic origin live in Kenya, mostly along the coastal strip.

Fort Jesus dominates the old town of Mombasa. It has witnessed much of Kenya's early history.

COLONIAL IMPACT

The majority of Europeans arrived nearly 200 years later, during the British colonial period when Kenya was known as the British East Africa Protectorate. The British decided to construct a railway from Mombasa, across Kenya and into Uganda to open up trade beyond the coastal strip. Work began in 1896, with the railway reaching Nairobi (then just a

The arrival of Kenya's railway system had an important impact on the country.

swamp) in 1899 and Kisumu on Lake Victoria by 1901. The railway was to change Kenya and its population forever. Britain invited people to Kenya to set up farms in the fertile highlands and grow crops for export to fund the construction of the railway. British settlers arrived in their thousands, displacing local people (especially the Kikuyu and Masai) to create massive colonial farms in an area that became known as the 'White Highlands'. Local people, annoyed at losing the most productive land to the Europeans, began a campaign of resistance. This eventually led to Kenya gaining independence in 1963, but at the invitation of Kenya's first president, Jomo Kenyatta, many Europeans stayed and today there are roughly 150,000 living in Kenya.

REDRAWING THE MAP

Mount Kilimanjaro was originally in British-controlled Kenya. In 1886 Queen Victoria gave it to her German cousin as a birthday present. The borders were re-drawn to include Kilimanjaro in German East Africa (now Tanzania).

As well as the arrival of Europeans, some 30,000 labourers were brought to Kenya from India to build the railway. Many of them stayed when their work was completed and set up businesses of their own. Today, the Indian population in Kenya is around 100,000, most of whom live in towns and cities along the route of the railway.

CASE STUDY
THE MAU MAU UPRISING

Mau Mau refers to a secret oath taken by members of the Land and Freedom Army, a group of mainly Kikuyu men determined to regain land which had been occupied by Europeans in the White Highlands. In the early 1950s, the struggle turned to violence, with attacks against white farms and Africans loyal to the British. In 1952, the government declared a state of emergency, calling in the British army,

rounding up Kikuyu people (and others) into controlled villages or camps, and arresting local political leaders (including Jomo Kenyatta), despite little evidence of their involvement. Tensions and conflict continued until 1960, by which time the Mau Mau Uprising had cost the lives of around 100 Europeans and 2,000 of their loyal supporters. The Mau Mau suffered around 11,000 deaths, but their struggle forced the British to consider the future of the colony and led to Kenya gaining its independence just three years later in 1963.

THE AFRICAN POPULATION

Although most of Kenya's population are black Africans, there are enormous differences within this grouping, the main divisions being by language group. Bantu speakers arrived in Kenya from the south and west over 1,000 years ago. The majority of this group are Kikuyu people. Nilotic speakers form the second main language group and arrived in Kenya 400–500 years ago from the Nile river basin to the north and west. Cushite speakers originating from modern-day Sudan, Ethiopia and Somalia are the third major language group. They arrived at a similar time to the Nilotic population. In total there are over 70 ethnic groups in Kenya and over 200 tribal languages are spoken. Swahili (a mixture of Bantu and Arabic languages) has become a common language for Kenya and is spoken by two thirds of people. Almost 10 per cent of Kenyans speak English.

Competition for land and resources has led to tensions between Kenya's ethnic groups. This problem was further enhanced when the first president, Jomo Kenyatta, favoured his own Kikuyu people above those from other ethnic backgrounds. This led to corruption within the government, which continues today with the Kikuyu and Kalenjin, (President Moi's own ethnic group), being the main beneficiaries.

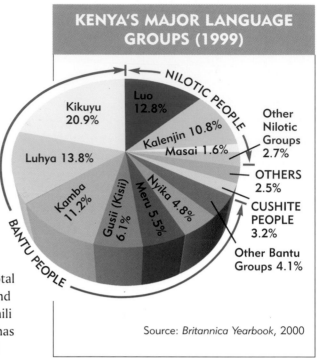

KENYA'S MAJOR LANGUAGE GROUPS (1999)

NILOTIC PEOPLE

Kikuyu 20.9%

Luo 12.8%

Kalenjin 10.8%

Masai 1.6%

Other Nilotic Groups 2.7%

OTHERS 2.5%

CUSHITE PEOPLE 3.2%

Other Bantu Groups 4.1%

Luhya 13.8%

Kamba 11.2%

Gusii (Kisii) 6.1%

Meru 5.5%

Nyika 4.8%

BANTU PEOPLE

Source: *Britannica Yearbook*, 2000

Opponents from other ethnic groups often find themselves ignored by the larger ethnic groups who are loyal to the ruling party. At a more local level, physical conflict between certain ethnic groups remains a problem for the government, despite its efforts to reduce such clashes. The north-west area of the country is particularly badly affected, with regular conflicts occuring between pastoral groups such as the Pokot, Turkana and Marakwet people.

Although the most famous of Kenya's people, the Masai are actually a relatively small ethnic group.

This has a long history, but in recent years has become more violent as herders have acquired guns from neighbouring Uganda and Sudan to protect their cattle.

Ethnic conflicts are greatest amongst Kenya's pastoral people, with cattle rustling being a particular problem.

POPULATION DISTRIBUTION AND DENSITY

Kenya's people are unevenly distributed, with the majority (around 70 per cent) living in the south-western corner; an area that includes the highlands, Lake Victoria and Nairobi. Much of the north of the country is sparsely populated, owing to its hostile climatic conditions. North Eastern Province, for example, contains just over 2 per cent of Kenya's population, yet makes up almost 22 per cent of Kenya's land area. By contrast, Nyanza Province, bordering Lake Victoria, covers just 2 per cent of Kenya, but is home to almost 17 per cent of its people, making it one of the most densely populated provinces.

Population density is important for the provision and maintenance of services such as electricity supplies, piped water, education and health centres. It is easier and cheaper to provide facilities in areas of high population density than in those that are sparsely populated. However, high population densities can be problematic if the region is unable to support so many people. Soil erosion, deforestation and water shortages are just three examples of problems facing Kenya's densely populated areas, but the biggest problems are often found in high density urban centres.

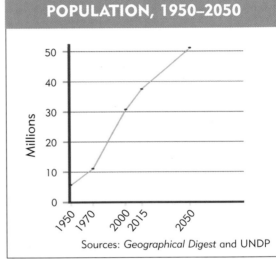

POPULATION, 1950–2050

Sources: *Geographical Digest* and UNDP

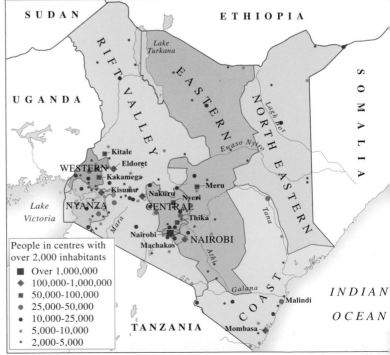

POPULATION DENSITY BY PROVINCE

People in centres with over 2,000 inhabitants
- ■ Over 1,000,000
- ◆ 100,000–1,000,000
- ■ 50,000–100,000
- ● 25,000–50,000
- ● 10,000–25,000
- ● 5,000–10,000
- · 2,000–5,000

URBANISATION

Kenya's urban population (like that of many developing countries) is growing at a faster rate than its national population. Land shortages in rural areas and the hope of employment and higher incomes in urban centres have led urban populations to grow at 7 per cent per year, about twice the national growth rate.

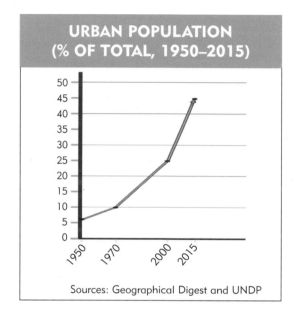

URBAN POPULATION (% OF TOTAL, 1950–2015)

Sources: Geographical Digest and UNDP

Such rapid urbanisation is problematic for city authorities as they struggle to keep pace with demand for housing, schools, healthcare and basic services, such as water and electricity supplies. People have resorted to developing their own settlements, many of which are now permanent communities. These shanty towns, or slums, are usually built of basic materials, such as iron sheets and wood or scrap materials that people can salvage from nearby. They are normally located on the edge of towns on land considered to be wasteland or unsuitable for housing. To the north of Nairobi for example, Mathare Valley shanty town is built along the swampy flood plain of the Mathare River. The shanty town lacks basic provisions such as clean water, sanitation and electricity, yet supports an estimated population of over 100,000 people.

THREATENED TRADITIONS

The mixing of Kenya's ethnic groups (especially in the cities) means that many traditions are becoming weaker and less practised, especially by younger generations. This decline is further influenced by Western culture. Even in remote parts of Kenya there is evidence of Western products and music. In fact in much of Kenya, many traditions such as costumes, dancing and singing are kept alive only as tourist attractions.

Rapid population growth leads to overcrowded, low-quality housing. This settlement is on the outskirts of Mombasa.

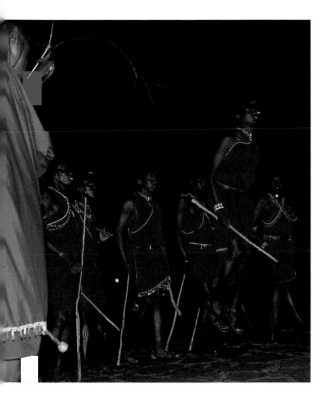

Such traditions may even be demonstrated by people who do not belong to that ethnic group, reducing them to little more than performances in a theme park. In other parts of the country, traditions remain strong, such as among the Masai who can still be seen herding their cattle wearing traditional dress. Where they have come into contact with tourists, however, such as in the Masai Mara and Amboseli National Parks, much of Masai life has become commercialised, with show villages and dance displays becoming a major source of income. In more remote parts of Kenya, away from Western influences and tourists, some groups still observe traditions and ceremonies. The rights of passage into adulthood are still routinely practised.

LEFT: Many traditions, such as Masai dancing, have been turned into commercial entertainments for tourists.

CASE STUDY
POKOT RIGHTS OF PASSAGE

The Pokot people of north-western Kenya still practise many of their traditions, one of the strongest being the right of passage into manhood. At a time decided by Pokot elders (about every seven years) all boys over the age of ten will complete their rights of passage. This involves being circumcised and spending a period of three months living in the bush learning skills such as hunting, building and fighting – skills that they will need as men. During this period they must not meet their mothers, and they wear a special head-dress made of goatskin and sisal, which hides their faces. When they are hungry, the boys sing and their mothers leave them food in the bush. The women wear bells so that the boys can follow them to collect the food without coming into contact with them. After three months the boys emerge as men and are given a special name to mark the occasion. The name relates to the year in which they became men. For example, those

A Pokot boy during the rights of passage.

with the name 'Kaperur' became men during a time of good rain, whilst those circumcised in the year the new road was built are named 'Sowo'. Such ceremonies and names are an important aspect of Kenyan culture and part of people's identity, but these traditions are under increasing threat from Western culture.

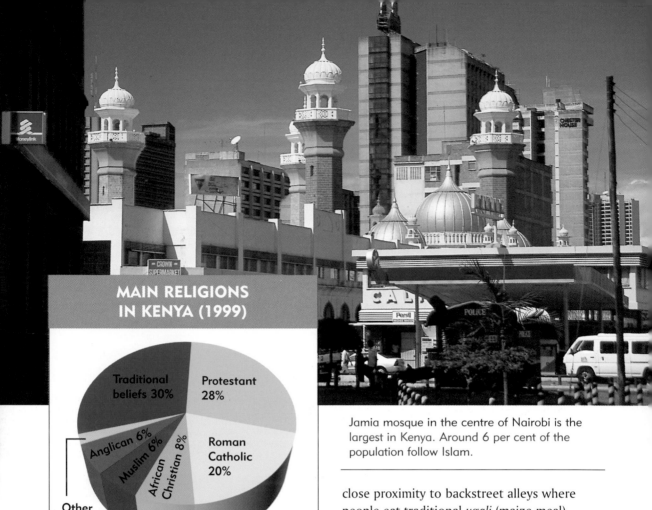

MAIN RELIGIONS IN KENYA (1999)

- Traditional beliefs 30%
- Protestant 28%
- Roman Catholic 20%
- African Christian 8%
- Anglican 6%
- Muslim 6%
- Other 2%

Source: *Britannica Yearbook*, 2000

Jamia mosque in the centre of Nairobi is the largest in Kenya. Around 6 per cent of the population follow Islam.

COSMOPOLITAN KENYA

The combination of historical and contemporary influences have created an extremely varied people and culture in modern-day Kenya. People of different ethnicity, different religions and different languages share each other's lives and work together in the spirit of *harambee* (pulling together) – the famous call of Jomo Kenyatta. In Nairobi, it is possible to see people from all sectors of society and experience the full range of Kenya's cosmopolitan culture. On the outskirts of the city, the Bomas of Kenya offer a glimpse of traditional life, whilst in the city centre, Internet cafés and mobile phones show Kenya's place in the world of high technology and global communications. Foreign burger and pizza outlets stand in close proximity to backstreet alleys where people eat traditional *ugali* (maize meal) and beans. Electrical stores sell the latest DVD players or computer games, whilst on the street corner a group of men may sit playing *bao*, a board game that has hardly changed for hundreds of years. The differences that make modern Kenya such a cosmopolitan country also make it a divided country, however, as not everyone shares equally in what is on offer.

DIVISIONS REMAIN

Despite the relative success of *harambee* in building a stable and peaceful society, there are enormous inequalities in virtually all aspects of Kenyan life. For the wealthy, Kenya offers luxury accommodation and endless opportunities. Enormous ranches mark the old colonial farms, many of them still occupied by Europeans and producing high-quality export produce. In urban centres, smart suburbs are full of grand houses, their privileged occupants protected by high walls, barbed-wire fences and security guards.

CASE STUDY
YOUTHFUL POPULATION

Over half of Kenya's population is under the age of 18, compared to just 26 per cent in the USA and 23 per cent in the UK. With so many young people, it is difficult to provide healthcare, education and employment for them all. Poorer parents cannot afford to care for all their children, leaving many children with little choice but to seek work to help provide for themselves. It is estimated that 40 per cent of 6–16-year-olds are in paid employment in Kenya, mainly working in the agriculture sector on tea, coffee, sugar cane or other plantations. Although this is contrary to their rights as a child and prevents them studying, they are better off than the increasing number of homeless children forced to beg on the streets for their survival.

One of the biggest problems is the lack of opportunities for young people. Many feel frustrated and this has led to an increase in crime, and violence between youth groups and the government. Improvements in healthcare and family planning mean that parents are having fewer children, but the difficulties of supporting and providing opportunities for such a young population are likely to remain for some time.

Street children are a sign of Kenya's inability to cope with such a youthful population.

Beyond the fences is a very different Kenya where people continue to live in poverty, in poor housing conditions, and with few basic facilities. More importantly perhaps, the differences between people are unevenly spread within the population as a whole. Recent estimates suggest that just 10 per cent of Kenyans own almost half the country's wealth, whilst 13 million people (about 43 per cent of the population) live and die in poverty.

Millions of Kenyan people continue to live very basic lifestyles, sharing little of their country's wealth.

KENYA'S ECONOMY

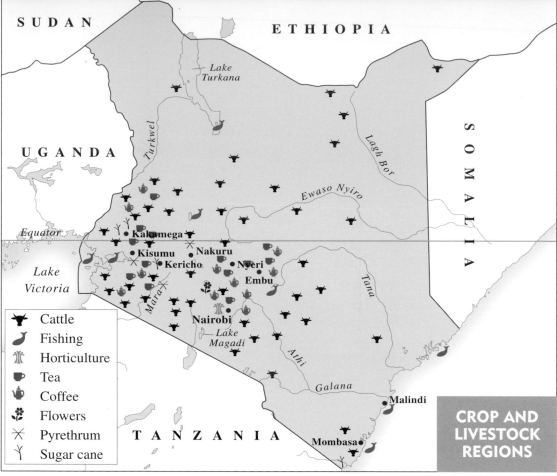

CROP AND LIVESTOCK REGIONS

Map legend:
- Cattle
- Fishing
- Horticulture
- Tea
- Coffee
- Flowers
- Pyrethrum
- Sugar cane

Labels on map: SUDAN, ETHIOPIA, UGANDA, SOMALIA, TANZANIA, Lake Turkana, Lake Victoria, Lake Magadi, Equator, Turkwel, Lagh Bor, Ewaso Nyiro, Mara, Tana, Athi, Galana, Kakamega, Kisumu, Nakuru, Kericho, Nyeri, Embu, Nairobi, Malindi, Mombasa

Kenya's economy relies heavily on agriculture for employment and income. This dependence is grounded in Kenya's colonial past, when large plantations and estates were established to grow cash crops for export back to Europe. Today, agriculture accounts for about a quarter of Kenya's domestic earnings (called its Gross Domestic Product, or GDP) though it is now a more diverse sector, with small-scale farmers playing as important a role as the large plantations and estates.

Kenya's main agricultural crops include tea, coffee, sugar cane, maize, wheat, beans and rice. Fruit and vegetables, flowers, and a special crop called pyrethrum (a plant containing a natural insecticide) are also significant contributors to the agricultural sector.

Hypericums are one of several flower types cultivated in Kenya's rapidly expanding floriculture industry.

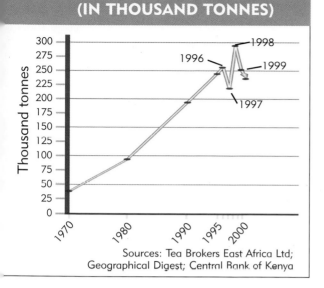

TEA PRODUCTION IN KENYA (IN THOUSAND TONNES)

Thousand tonnes

300
275 — 1998
250 — 1996 — 1999
225
200 — 1997
175
150
125
100
75
50
25
0

1970 1980 1990 1995 2000

Sources: Tea Brokers East Africa Ltd;
Geographical Digest; Central Bank of Kenya

TEA – A CASH CROP

Tea is Kenya's primary cash crop and competes with tourism as Kenya's largest source of foreign earnings. In 1996 Kenya became the world's leading tea exporter for the first time, although it has since fallen back to the third-largest behind its main competitors – India and Sri Lanka. Tea estates were introduced to the western side of the Great Rift Valley around the 1920s. This area has near-perfect growing conditions for tea, with cool temperatures at an altitude of between 1,000 and 2,000m, regular rainfall of at least 100mm per month, and acidic, well-drained soils.

Tea picking is labour intensive and the industry and related services employ an estimated 1 million Kenyans. Many work in large tea estates owned by multinational companies such as Brooke Bond. There are 58 tea estates in Kenya, accounting for around 30 per cent of the area planted with tea and 46 per cent of tea production. This relatively high level of production is due to the more intensive production methods used by the estates. In comparison, the 270,000 smallholder tea growers who make up the balance of Kenya's tea growers account for 70 per cent of the area planted, but only 54 per cent of production. With its reputation for high quality tea, Kenya is likely to remain a major world producer and the area cultivated is still expanding.

CASE STUDY
BROOKE BOND TEA ESTATE, KERICHO

At Brooke Bond's Kericho estates, teams of around 70 pickers work an area of tea, picking just the fresh tips (2 leaves and a bud) from each bush. These are then dried, crushed, shredded and repeatedly fermented to produce tea leaves ready for export – called 'made tea'. For every 100kg of leaves roughly 22.5kg of made tea will be produced. The picking teams rotate around the estate, returning to the same bushes approximately every thirteen days, by which time the tips have regrown. A normal working day is seven hours, for which pickers were paid a minimum of 136K Sh in 2001 providing they had picked at least 33kg of quality tea.

In addition to their pay, workers are provided with housing, schooling for their children, and healthcare and medical facilities for their whole family.

Plantation workers are highly skilled at picking just the tips needed for making tea.

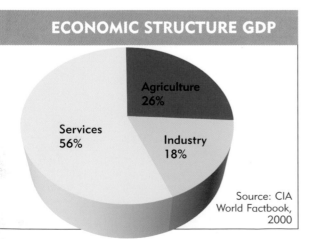

The beaches around Mombasa attract most of Kenya's tourists.

TOURISM

The combination of tropical beaches and spectacular wildlife make Kenya an ideal tourist destination. Visitor numbers have grown rapidly from just 61,000 at independence to 1,003,000 in 1996, turning tourism into a vital sector of Kenya's economy, accounting for around 19 per cent of GDP. However, security concerns, such as pre-election violence in 1997 and the bombing of the American embassy in Nairobi in August 1998, which killed 263 people, have caused a sudden downturn in tourism. In 1998, just 894,300 tourists visited Kenya – a 10.8 per cent decline in just two years. Competition from other tourist destinations (especially South Africa), an ageing infrastructure (airports, roads, hotels etc) and the re-introduction of visa charges in March 2001,

meant that Kenya's tourist industry was struggling to recover its visitor numbers in 2001. However, tourism remains one of the country's largest foreign-exchange earners and employs at least 100,000 people. Although much of this employment is provided directly by hotels and tour companies, many more find indirect employment as a result of the tourist industry. In almost every town and near every major attraction curio shops sell handicrafts, postcards and other tourist merchandise. Restaurants and bars provide refreshments, snacks and meals, and companies provide many services, from car hire to coral diving and mountain trekking. A large informal sector also exists with hawkers patrolling beaches and hotels selling souvenirs or offering excursions to tourists. On Mombasa's beaches this hawking has become so widespread that hotel owners and the council have enforced new rules to prevent tourists being hassled.

THE MOVE TOWARDS ECO-TOURISM

Not everyone, however, benefits from tourism. About 70 per cent of the largest and most popular tourist operations are owned by foreign interests, meaning that profits often go overseas. Many tourists stay strictly within the hotel resorts, so few local people benefit from their presence. Those that do benefit are often in poorly paid unskilled jobs, such as hotel porters and cleaners.

ECONOMIC STRUCTURE GDP

Agriculture 26%

Services 56%

Industry 18%

Source: CIA World Factbook, 2000

In fact, the difference between the luxury tourist resorts and life for those living just beyond their boundaries is often worlds apart. In the best resorts tourists can pay an average Kenyan's annual earnings (around US$350) for a single night! In recognition of this problem efforts are now being made to develop tourism in partnership with local communities, especially around the main national parks. In these areas people became so frustrated at not sharing in the income generated by tourism that, in protest, they even took to killing the wildlife that tourists came to see. When Amboseli National Park was created in 1973 and the Masai were told they could no longer graze their cattle there, they all but killed off the black rhino (the park's emblem), and so damaged the lion population that it has never fully recovered. The Masai now work more closely with the Kenya Wildlife Service, but some still feel sidelined by tourism.

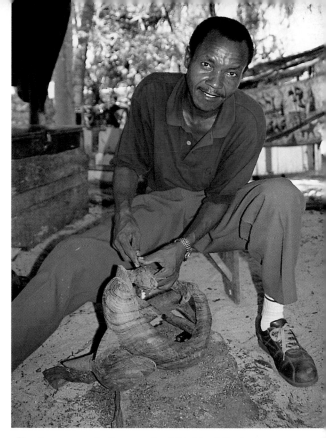

Tourism supports thousands of highly skilled craftspeople.

DIVERSIFYING THE ECONOMY

One of Kenya's main challenges is to move away from its dependence on agriculture and tourism. Tourist numbers can fluctuate dramatically and relying on one or two agricultural commodities makes Kenya vulnerable to world price changes. For example tea prices increased by almost 25 per cent between 1997 and 1998, in this instance benefiting Kenya, but they could just as easily fall by a similar (or greater) amount in a single year. Kenya's industrial sector expanded rapidly in the 1990s as economic policies made it easier for foreign investors to establish businesses. In 1990, just 8 per cent of GDP was generated by industry, but this had increased to 14 per cent by 1995 and was approaching 20 per cent by 2000.

Safari tourists hope to see the 'big five' (lion, rhino, leopard, elephant and buffalo). These tourist have spotted some lions on the ridge.

KAM 381D

INDUSTRIAL EXPORTS

Principal industrial exports include petroleum products (refined at Mombasa), cement, soda ash and fluorite. In the manufacturing sector food processing, metal products, vehicle assembly, beverage and textile production are all major industries, many of them located in the industrial zones of Nairobi and Mombasa. The service sector, including banking, insurance and other business services, has expanded with the general growth in the economy. One service industry that has grown particularly fast is real estate, reflecting Kenya's rapid urbanisation and continued population growth. If tourism is included, the service sector generates over half of Kenya's GDP and is likely to expand further to support the rapid growth in telecommunications and computer use.

Roses, being packed here for export to Europe, are one of Kenya's most valuable products.

KENYA'S MAJOR TRADING PARTNERS (% GDP) 1998

EXPORTS

- Uganda 16%
- UK 13%
- Tanzania 13%
- Egypt 5%
- Germany 5%
- Other 48%

IMPORTS

- UK 12%
- UAE 9%
- US 8%
- Japan 8%
- Germany 6%
- India 4%
- Other 47%

Source: CIA World Factbook 2000

NEW OPPORTUNITIES

Traditional sectors of the economy, such as agriculture and tourism, are having to adapt to new economic conditions in a more globally integrated and competitive world. One agricultural sector that has proved particularly successful at this is horticulture – the growing of fruit, vegetables and flowers. Three crucial factors enabled Kenya to take advantage of the growing market for horticultural produce in northern Europe:

- near optimum climatic conditions for growing horticultural produce;
- a cheap and plentiful supply of labour;
- strong trading links with Europe, especially historical links with the UK.

Foreign investors were quick to establish large farms in Kenya and horticulture grew rapidly during the 1980s and 1990s. It is now one of the most important agricultural sectors, having overtaken coffee as Kenya's second most valuable agricultural earner after tea. The opening of Eldoret airport in 1999 offers improved transport links for exporting horticultural produce and is expected to lead to further expansion in the industry. Some believe horticulture could soon replace tea and tourism as Kenya's main earner of foreign revenue if it continues to grow at present rates.

ECONOMIC SLOWDOWN

Despite its success in diversification and long-term growth in key sectors such as tea, horticulture and tourism, Kenya's economy has been slowing since its peak growth period in the 1970s. The 1990s has been Kenya's slowest decade of growth since independence, with 1993 actually seeing a decline in economic growth for the first time since 1970. This slowdown in the economy is of particular concern to Kenya because of its continued high population growth. If this is taken into account then the economy barely kept ahead of population during the 1980s and has

Much of Kenya's trade takes place through Mombasa port. This ship is waiting to load with cement.

actually failed to keep pace with population throughout the 1990s. In real terms this means that Kenya had a Gross National Product (GNP) per capita of US$350 in 1998, an improvement on just US$260 in 1995, but significantly below the high of US$450 achieved in 1980.

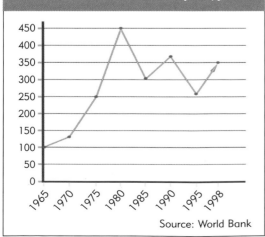

GNP PER CAPITA (US$)

Source: World Bank

EMPLOYMENT

The combination of a slowing economy and growing population means that the level of unemployment is a major concern in Kenya. In 1998, the unemployment rate was estimated to be 50 per cent. Of those who were employed about 60 per cent are thought to work in the informal sector. This sector plays an important role in providing jobs and developing people's skills, but with the population growing at 2.3 per cent per year, Kenya's economy must perform better to avoid unemployment increasing further still.

Employment in Kenya is very difficult to measure as many people are engaged in subsistence livelihoods, such as farming, pastoralism and fishing, providing for their own needs rather than earning money to meet them. Those in the subsistence sector are often ignored in employment figures, despite their importance to the Kenyan economy. For example, 70 per cent of the country's coffee is produced by small-scale producers, and many of these are subsistence farmers.

FEMALE LABOUR FORCE (% OF TOTAL)

Year	%
1965	45.1
1975	45.6
1985	46.0
1995	46.1
1998	46.1

Sources: ILO (International Labour Organisation)

INFRASTRUCTURE

Without a good infrastructure it is difficult for an economy to function and grow. Roads and railways provide vital links for trade, whilst electricity and telephone networks deliver the power and communications needed for businesses to develop. Kenya faces problems in all these areas. The transport network has suffered from a lack of government investment and poor maintenance over the years.

CASE STUDY
JUA KALI – THE INFORMAL SECTOR

The *jua kali* sector teaches skills such as mechanics to unemployed young people.

Jua kali is the name given to Kenya's small-scale informal sector. It means 'fierce sun' and refers to the fact that many people in this sector work outside. *Jua kali* developed from traditional skills such as pottery, metal working, basketry and weaving, and today produces goods such as metal window frames and gates, cooking stoves and furniture. It also offers services such as welding, tailoring and mechanics workshops. In recent years the *jua kali* sector has been recognised for the important role it plays in employment, training and the production of affordably priced goods for the local market. The skills learnt in the *jua kali* sector are essential to Kenya's continued industrialisation and economic growth.

ELECTRICITY GENERATION (1998)

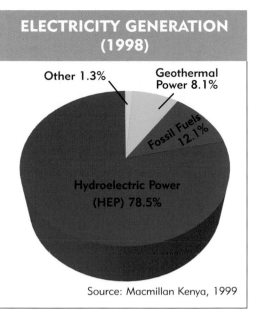

Other 1.3%

Geothermal Power 8.1%

Fossil Fuels 12.1%

Hydroelectric Power (HEP) 78.5%

Source: Macmillan Kenya, 1999

KEY ROADS, RAILWAY LINES, AIRPORTS AND PORTS

The railway is now used mainly for freight, with the last major passenger route between Nairobi and Mombasa being reduced from a daily service to just three times a week in March 2001. Only 14 per cent of roads are tarred, the majority are earthen. During the rainy seasons many earthen roads become impassable, cutting off large sections of the country. Tarred roads are poorly maintained, with potholes and cracked surfaces making driving conditions hazardous and causing damage to vehicles. In terms of electricity, Kenya was forced to introduce rationing, with 12-hour power cuts for six days a week in May–November 2000.

This was due to prolonged drought affecting water levels in Kenya's hydroelectric dams on which it depends for over 75 per cent of its power generation. New dams and an extension to Olkaria geothermal power station are being developed to prevent this problem recurring, but power generation is likely to remain a major challenge for Kenya's growing economy.

The Trans-African Highway connects Kenya to its neighbours and is vital to the economy.

PROGRESS IN DEVELOPMENT

It is difficult to meet the needs of a population with so many children.

Kenya is the seventeenth-poorest country in the world, with about half the population living on less than US$1 a day. Social development in areas such as education and health is also poor and in some cases is actually deteriorating. Yet progress has been made. Since independence Kenya's child mortality rate has almost halved (although it is still high at 117 deaths for every 1,000 children born) and adult literacy has nearly doubled to 80.5 per cent of the population. Improvements in life expectancy, however, have been slower, mainly as a result of HIV/AIDS.

Awareness of family planning is considered essential to reducing population growth.

POPULATION GROWTH

One of the greatest challenges to development in Kenya is its rapid rate of population growth. Between 1970 and 1990 Kenya's population grew at a rate of about 3.6 per cent per year, making it one of the fastest-growing populations in the world. Such rapid population growth makes it difficult to keep pace with the provision of services such as schools and hospitals, water and sanitation, housing and transport facilities. Population growth fell to 2.6 per cent in the 1990s.

This figure is expected to fall to just 1.5 per cent per year for the period 2000–2015, but the provision of services will remain a challenge because of Kenya's population momentum. This refers to the process whereby although population growth rates may decrease, the actual number of people added to the population remains high for some time due to the youthful nature of the population structure. In Kenya's case, 51.8 per cent of the population was under 18 years of age in 1998, most of whom will not yet have started their own families. Providing healthcare facilities that allow people to choose the size of their families is therefore a major development target. Improving child survival rates and the rate of contraceptive use (currently just 33 per cent) are two such measures that could drastically reduce the pressure of continued population growth on Kenya's environment and economy. Central to both of these aims is education, especially the education of girls.

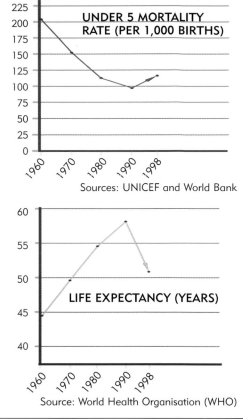

UNDER 5 MORTALITY RATE (PER 1,000 BIRTHS)

Sources: UNICEF and World Bank

LIFE EXPECTANCY (YEARS)

Source: World Health Organisation (WHO)

CASE STUDY
THE SPREAD OF HIV/AIDS

Tumia Mpira
UKIMWI HUUA

ANYBODY CAN GET

AIDS KILLS
Use Condoms

AIDS

TAKE CARE

These posters at a vegetable farm warn workers about the risk of HIV/AIDS.

Life expectancy in Kenya fell from 57 years to 51 years over the period 1990–98. This dramatic fall is almost entirely due to the devastating effect of HIV/AIDS, which claims around 500 Kenyan lives each day. In fact, without HIV/AIDS it is estimated that life expectancy would have been 64 years in 1998 – 13 years higher than it actually was. Kenya would today have over 1 million more people than it does with the HIV/AIDS problem. About 14 per cent of Kenyans (4.2 million) are infected with the virus and the number is growing daily. In fact the disease is almost out of control, with AIDS patients occupying half of the country's already overstretched hospital beds. Since HIV/AIDS has the biggest impact on the most economically active people in society (15–45-year-olds), it is also affecting the economy and leaving thousands of families without their main income earner. In 2000 the Kenyan government declared HIV/AIDS a national disaster. Many feel this was 15 years too late and that more should have been done to prevent the spread of the disease in the past.

EDUCATION FOR ALL

Education is considered essential for the development of a country, providing the skills and knowledge that will allow it to succeed in other development objectives. The United Nations (UN) has made education for all children (to at least the end of primary school) an international development target to be met by the year 2015. The education of girls is considered especially important as it is known that an educated woman is likely to have fewer, healthier children than an uneducated woman. In Kenya, primary education is technically free, but because government funding is unable to meet the total cost of learning materials and buildings, parents have to make up the difference by paying school fees. In recent years government funding for education has decreased due to economic reforms. Combined with slower economic growth and persistent poverty, this has caused the number of children being enrolled in school to fall significantly.

In the early 1990s, 85 per cent of school-age children were enrolled in primary school, but by 1999–2000 figures suggested this had fallen to below 60 per cent, meaning that 2.5 million school-age children were not attending school. Even where children are able to attend school, only around 40 per cent of them will actually manage to complete their primary schooling.

The education of girls is considered vital to the future development of Kenya.

EDUCATION FOR GIRLS

Where families have limited funds available for education, they will often choose to send boys, believing that their education is more valuable than that of girls. For example, at secondary level over one in four boys are likely to attend, whereas it is nearer one in five for girls. Throughout Kenya, a relatively high proportion of non-attendees and drop-outs are girls, but this is especially so in more remote areas, where cultural beliefs about women's roles in society remain stronger.

Regular health checks for infants have helped to halve child mortality since independence.

HEALTH OF THE NATION

As Kenya's low life expectancy and high child mortality suggests, healthcare in Kenya is an area in need of urgent improvement. With only fifteen doctors for every 100,000 people, compared to 164 in the UK and 245 in the USA, Kenya is extremely short of trained medical staff. This situation is aggravated by the fact that 80 per cent of doctors are based in urban centres, whilst 70 per cent of the population still live in rural areas. For over half of these people the nearest health centre is over 4km away and a quarter of Kenyans must travel over 8km to seek medical attention. The introduction of fees for healthcare has left many Kenyans unable to afford medical services and they are turning to traditional medicine as a cheaper alternative.

Local healers use their knowledge of plants (normally leaves, bark and roots) to prepare medicines for everything from stomach upsets to malaria. There is often conflict between supporters of traditional and modern medicine, but in some rural areas both methods are being used together in an effort to improve rural health services. In West Pokot District, for example, traditional healers are being trained by hospitals as birth attendants to assist women who are unable to reach the hospital.

One of the greatest challenges for Kenya is to invest more money in preventative healthcare such as immunisation programmes and health education. At present over 70 per cent of the health budget is spent on curative healthcare, much of which could be avoided if people were better able to prevent those illnesses in the first instance. Programmes such as 'Kick Polio out of Africa' have proven very successful and if combined with greater health awareness, such as the importance of personal hygiene, they are likely to relieve the pressure on Kenya's health services. One of the most effective ways to improve people's health is to improve basic living conditions.

Immunisation programmes can drastically reduce diseases, but health centres are desperately short of medical supplies.

WATER AND SANITATION

Safe water is a basic requirement for a healthy life and yet 56 per cent of Kenya's population have no access to it. Given that 80 per cent of illness in the world is a result of drinking contaminated water, this has serious implications for the health of Kenya's people. Diarrhoea is a big killer (especially of young children), even though death can normally be prevented by taking a simple mixture of sugar and salt. However, diarrhoea is likely to recur until there is a safe supply of water to prevent

Some of the worst water and sanitation problems are in urban areas. These open drains are in Eldoret.

further contamination. Kenya's biggest killer, malaria, is also related to water because the mosquitoes that carry the malaria parasite require water to breed. Where water is collected and stored in open containers it encourages mosquitoes to breed, leading to higher rates of malaria. Simple measures such as covering storage containers can dramatically reduce the risk of catching malaria.

Water is often contaminated as a result of poor sanitation. Sewers can leak or overflow into water supplies and in many rural areas, where proper toilets are often lacking, human waste is simply washed into local streams, contaminating the water for those collecting it further downstream. Providing a safe water supply can be extremely expensive and requires regular maintenance. But simple measures such as boiling drinking water and constructing pit-latrines (toilets) to contain waste away from water sources can have a dramatic impact. Basic hygiene such as washing hands before drinking or eating and after going to the toilet can also lead to significant reductions in certain water-related diseases.

DEBT AND DEVELOPMENT

Like many developing countries, Kenya has large debts as a result of borrowing money to assist in its development. In 1998, Kenya's

In many rural areas the majority of people still rely on rivers for their water supply.

debt stood at US$7 billion, equivalent to 61.5 per cent of GNP. Around 20 per cent of foreign earnings are spent paying off this debt; money that could otherwise be spent on improving basic provisions such as healthcare and education. Many of those concerned with poverty believe that great progress could be made if these debts were written off, allowing the Kenyan government to invest money in development instead of debt repayments. However, others point to inefficient government spending and corruption, blaming these factors for the slow progress in development. They suggest that until corruption is reduced, any money made available as a result of debt relief would be in danger of being used to further benefit those who are already better off.

CASE STUDY
SELF-HELP GROUPS

The Machakos District self-help group market their wares at an exhibition in Nairobi.

A feature of Kenya's development has been its self-help groups, often referred to locally as *harambee* groups. In the absence of government support, people all over the country have formed co-operatives, associations and organisations to work together towards common goals. Some groups are simple farmers' co-operatives, where farmers join together to purchase inputs such as seed and fertilisers in bulk and combine their produce to get the best possible prices at market. Others are more complex such as irrigation committees that share the costs and management of an irrigation scheme. Women in particular have benefited from self-help groups as they provide them with a voice in an otherwise male dominated society. One such group is the Machakos District Co-operative Union Ltd. Started in 1988, the co-operative now has 13 sub-groups with around 50 women in each using their spare time to make baskets, necklaces and other artefacts for sale. As a member of the International Federation of Alternative Trade they export their products to Europe and Japan, as well as selling them in Kenya. The profits are used to provide clothing, water pumps and maize mills for the women's home villages. Such groups not only improve local development but empower women, and provide people with a sense of self-esteem and pride.

THE ENVIRONMENT

Once cleared of forest, soils are vulnerable to rapid erosion from wind and water.

Much of Kenya's economy and most of its population are directly dependent on the state of the environment. Historically the environment has been able to support human activities, but there are signs that the fragile balance between people and their environment is being upset. Forest cover is disappearing, erosion is accelerating, watercourses are drying up, pollution incidents are increasing and wildlife numbers are declining in many species.

As well as damaging the environment, such changes affect people's livelihoods and well-being. If soils erode or water supplies run short then agriculture suffers, whilst any decline in wildlife populations could damage the country's tourist industry. Meeting people's needs without degrading the environment for future generations is one of the greatest challenges facing Kenya in the early twenty-first century. This challenge is known as sustainable development and focuses on restoring the balance between people and environments.

FOREST LOSS

Ever since the early colonial period when European settlers cleared vast tracts of forest to establish tea or coffee plantations, Kenya's forest cover has been declining at an alarming rate. At independence, forests made up about 30 per cent of Kenya's land area, but by 2000 this had been reduced to less than 3 per cent. Forest is cleared for a number of reasons, but clearance for agricultural land or for providing wood for fuel or charcoal are often the main causes. High population growth combined with a shortage of productive agricultural land has led to areas of forest being cleared and occupied by squatters. In 2001, the government announced plans to clear a further 10 per cent of the country's remaining forests to provide land for such people, but these plans have met with strong resistance. Many believe they are another example of government corruption and that the forest areas will be given as rewards to important government supporters. The poor and landless, they say, will not benefit from these plans.

There are also concerns over the environmental impact of such projects because the planned forest clearances include five of the country's main water catchments.

The tree cover in these areas helps store water and release it gradually into the nation's rivers and lakes over the year. It is estimated that the five catchments planned for clearance provide 90 per cent of the country's domestic water supply, 70 per cent of the water used to generate hydroelectric power and much of the country's irrigation water. With tree cover removed, there are concerns that water shortages, power cuts and falling agricultural production will follow. Springs and rivers around Lake Nakuru and the Mount Kenya region are already drying up, following forest clearances begun in 1994. Experts say that further clearance of catchments around Nakuru could lead to Lake Nakuru, one of the most important natural habitats and Kenya's most visited national park, drying up altogether.

Commercial logging supplies wood for the construction industry and paper mills.

CASE STUDY
GREEN BELT MOVEMENT

Workers at this tree nursery prepare seedlings for sale and distribution to local farmers.

In 1977, a biologist called Wangari Maathai founded the Green Belt Movement as a reaction to the problems of forest loss, soil erosion and environmental damage in Kenya. Working with women's groups, the Green Belt Movement encouraged tree planting and greater awareness of the importance of trees in protecting the environment. They have since planted over 12 million trees across Kenya and beyond, and are involved with over 6,000 women's groups in a wide number of environmental campaigns. The Green Belt Movement has become internationally recognised and Wangari Maathai continues to lead it, despite being arrested and beaten by government forces on several occasions. She has been awarded the UN's Africa Prize for Leadership and some even believe that Wangari Maathai could become Kenya's (and Africa's) first female leader. For now, however, she is content to keep fighting for Kenya's environment and is currently teaching people how to protect their forest resources legally from further exploitation.

SOIL EROSION

Closely related to forest loss is the problem of soil erosion. Tree cover protects soils from heavy eroding rain, and tree roots help to hold soils together. If vegetation is removed, then erosion can be extremely rapid, forming enormous gullies or washing away whole fields in a single storm. Over-cultivation or over-grazing of livestock are the main causes of vegetation loss and subsequent erosion, but there are less obvious causes, too, such as tourism. In national parks, erosion is a major problem caused by the high number of tourist vehicles, which in the Masai Mara alone increased from 20,000 to 60,000 a year between 1986 and 1998. During the rainy seasons some areas of the park become impassable and in the dry seasons thick clouds of red dust spew into the sky as tourists rush to spot the next lion or elephant. Erosion is made even worse when tourists drive off-road to get closer to the wildlife. In several parks, off-road driving has now been banned, but these rules are often ignored by tourists and the parks are too big to patrol effectively.

Agriculture, however, is the biggest victim of erosion. As soils disappear, so do the nutrients essential for growing crops or sustaining grazing lands. Throughout Kenya agricultural production is declining as a result of erosion and poor soil fertility. However, this process is

preventable and, in some cases, reversible. Planting trees and terracing steep land are two measures that could be taken to reduce erosion and increase water retention in the soils. Growing a variety of crops (intercropping) instead of a single crop also reduces erosion because the different maturing times of the crops mean that the soil is covered with vegetation for a greater period of the year.

Soil erosion is one of Kenya's biggest problems. Huge gullies can appear in a short space of time.

Tourist vehicles leave trails of dust in their wake as the tourists rush to see the wildlife.

Terracing of hillsides reduces erosion and helps to capture and store water in the soils.

Intercropping with certain crops can also improve soil fertility. Beans and peas, for example, are leguminous plants, meaning they absorb nitrogen (an important fertiliser) from the atmosphere and fix it in the soils. Where intercropping with leguminous plants has been combined with terracing or tree planting, crop yields have increased dramatically, and the variety of crops provides improved diets and produces higher value surpluses for sale.

WATER POLLUTION

In a country already short of water, pollution of watercourses and groundwater is a serious concern. Industrial activity, improper disposal of domestic waste, and chemical run-off from agriculture are all significant causes of water pollution in Kenya. Among the most threatened water resources are the rift valley lakes of Naivasha and Nakuru. Lake Naivasha is an important freshwater resource supporting a local population of over 250,000 and numerous important industries, including Kenya's only geothermal power station and several floriculture farms. Flower farms pose a particular threat to the lake as they extract large volumes of water for use in irrigation and use high quantities of agrochemicals that can leach into groundwater and find their way back into the lake ecosystem. In recent years flower growers have implemented several measures to reduce their impact on Lake Naivasha. These include the introduction of drip irrigation systems to reduce water usage and lower pesticide use, combined with soak-pits to trap chemical run-off before it enters water systems.

Expensive irrigation equipment has helped to reduce the use of fertilisers in flower farms around Lake Naivasha.

A THREATENED HABITAT

For Lake Nakuru the main threat comes from nearby industries and waste from Nakuru town. The town dump is located on a geological fault that allows leachate (liquid waste) from the dump to find its way into the groundwater supplies that support the lake and its wildlife. As a result of weak restrictions on waste dumping, the leachate contains high quantities of chemicals and heavy metals, some of which are highly toxic to people and wildlife. Tests on boreholes in the area have shown high levels of lead in the water, whilst the lake waters themselves show high concentrations of lead, mercury, chromium and arsenic. In 1999, thousands of flamingos that rely on Lake Nakuru for feeding, fell sick and died. Tests on their bodies revealed high levels of metal poisoning as the cause of their death and led to calls for dumps to be relocated and industries to dispose of their wastes more carefully. Thankfully the lake's health has improved since 1999, and in 2001 flamingos began nesting at Nakuru for the first time since 1935. However, water pollution remains a problem and smaller numbers of flamingos are still falling sick after feeding at Nakuru.

URBAN ENVIRONMENTS

With a rapidly growing urban population, environmental problems in urban areas are becoming increasingly evident. One of the more obvious problems is waste disposal.

Roadsides within all but the wealthiest urban areas are littered with rubbish containing anything from food scraps and newspapers to hazardous wastes, such as old batteries, and chemical products. As well as the risk of contaminating watercourses, such waste heaps encourage vermin, present a human health hazard, and block drains and gullies, which leads to flooding during the rains. Communities attempt to solve these problems by burning the waste, but this releases toxic fumes into the air, many of which are hazardous to human health, or emit ozone-destroying CFCs.

MAIN PICTURE: Flamingos have proven highly vulnerable to industrial pollution. INSET: These vehicles being washed in Lake Victoria are releasing pollutants into the lake ecosystem.

CASE STUDY
WATER HYACINTH

The water hyacinth first appeared in Lake Victoria in 1989, having floated down the Kagera River from Rwanda, where it is thought to have been introduced as an ornamental plant from South America. It spread rapidly, finding the conditions in Lake Victoria ideal. By 1996 the water hyacinth had become a major problem, choking waterways, closing fishing beaches and stranding cargo boats. Expensive machines were introduced to harvest the weed. Plans were also made to destroy it using chemical herbicides, but there were concerns that this might harm Kenya's profitable fish export industry. In the end a solution came from a less obvious source – a small South American weevil (*Brochi Neochetina*). First discovered by Australian scientists, the weevil was found to have an enormous appetite for the hyacinth plant and its larvae destroyed the growth of the plant by burrowing into it. Introduced in 1997, the tiny weevils had destroyed 80 per cent of the water hyacinth by mid-2000, allowing lake activities to return to normal. However, patches of weed were returning to Uganda's share of Lake Victoria in early 2001, suggesting that Kenya's struggle to control water hyacinth is not yet over.

The water hyacinth (in the foreground) has caused major problems for the lake economy, blocking landing sites and disrupting transport.

Roadside burning of waste is unhygienic and adds to urban air pollution.

A POSITIVE SOLUTION

Some organisations are trying to tackle the problem of waste disposal. The City Garbage Recyclers, based in Maringo Estate, Nairobi, have come up with an innovative approach. They collect waste and turn it into cheap, useable products that not only reduce waste, but also help to protect environmental resources. For example, waste paper and cartons are pulped and mixed with charcoal dust and then formed into fuel bricks for sale.

Useful materials are often recycled. These sandals have been made from old car tyres.

These are cheaper and more efficient than charcoal and reduce the pressure on forest resources. The waste paper is collected by street children, who are paid by the kilo, generating income for one of the most vulnerable groups in society. Another successful project is the recycling of old plastic bags. The bags are shredded and used as a stuffing to make cheap mattresses for Nairobi's urban poor. Such projects are still limited, but City Garbage Recyclers is encouraging other communities to set up similar schemes by increasing people's awareness of waste problems and providing training in recycling techniques.

WILDLIFE CONSERVATION AND TOURISM

Despite its significance to the economy, Kenya's wildlife is threatened by expanding human activities and competition for land and resources. Tourism, which is largely generated by the presence of wildlife, is in itself a significant threat. The thousands of foreign visitors who arrive each year require accommodation, food and water, transportation and luxury facilities such as swimming pools. In the Masai Mara for example, the number of tourists increased from 95,000 in 1986 to 332,000 by 1998. This 250 per cent increase in visitors has led to the construction of 21 new lodges and camps, several new airstrips and countless new tracks and access roads.

Lodges built in the middle of national parks place additional pressure on local wildlife.

Such developments disrupt animal movements, destroy or disturb habitats, and may cause excessive use of local resources. In Shaba National Reserve (north of Nairobi), springs used by the local Samburu people and wildlife have been diverted to provide water for a luxury hotel complex. In the Mara there is evidence to suggest that cheetahs are changing their normal hunting patterns as a result of tourist disruption, threatening the survival of their cubs. Instead of their normal dawn or dusk hunt, the cheetahs have switched to midday hunts when tourists are resting inside their luxury camps. For the cheetahs, this means using far more energy in the midday heat, reducing the chance of a successful hunt.

Not all tourism is damaging, however, and were it not for the income that wildlife tourism generates it is possible that Kenya's wildlife would be under much greater pressure, with some species such as the black rhino probably being extinct.

PLANTING TREES

In recent years, tourism companies have become increasingly aware of their impact on the environment and many have introduced policies to reduce this and assist in wildlife and habitat conservation. One of the most ambitious plans is the Amboseli Reforestation Project, which hopes to plant a million acacia trees over the next 30–50 years to restore the landscape to how it looked in the early 1900s – before major human impacts. Co-ordinated by two of the main tourist companies, the plan is to invite each tourist visiting the park to plant a tree, giving something back to the environment they have come to enjoy. In return they will receive a conservation certificate acknowledging their support.

Harambee groups, such as this irrigation committee, play an increasingly important role in building Kenya's future.

REVIVING *HARAMBEE*

Kenya faces many challenges as it enters the twenty-first century, but perhaps one of the most important is to revive the spirit of *harambee*. The corruption, inequality and ethnic divides that mark much of modern Kenya are a long way from the intentions of working together, represented by *harambee*. Until Kenya's people learn to trust each other and work towards the same goals, the future will remain difficult.

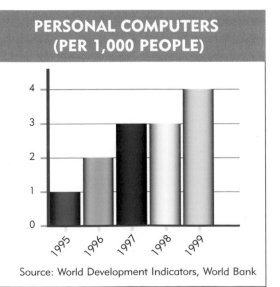

PERSONAL COMPUTERS (PER 1,000 PEOPLE)

Source: World Development Indicators, World Bank

There are examples of where this is already happening, such as increased co-operation between tour operators, the Kenya Wildlife Service (KWS) and local people in new eco-tourism projects. Such projects allow everyone to benefit from Kenya's wildlife, instead of limiting the benefits to a few individuals and foreign companies. The government must take a leading role in reviving *harambee* and lead by example, stamping out corruption and supporting local development initiatives. This is especially important in the run-up to the next elections in late 2002. The last two elections led to violence and ethnic tensions, causing great harm to Kenya's reputation as one of Africa's most peaceful and stable countries.

KENYA IN THE GLOBAL ECONOMY

Kenya, like all other countries, operates as part of an increasingly global economy; an economy that is characterised by modern communications, improved transportation and international trade links. However, the global economy is highly competitive, with companies able to relocate in, or buy products from whichever country offers them the best deal. Kenya must work hard to maintain its position as one of the most favoured locations in Africa, but this will mean improving services essential to modern business, such as transport networks, power supplies and telecommunications. There are signs that this is starting to happen. Roads connecting key urban centres are being repaired or upgraded, new power stations are being constructed and existing ones extended, and a revolution in mobile telecommunications is allowing previously remote parts of the country to become more accessible.

RIGHT: Modern communications such as the Internet and mobile phones provide support for new businesses.

CASE STUDY
AN ECO-TOURISM PROJECT

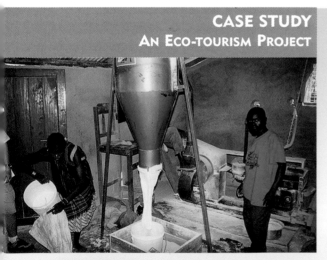

This grain mill was paid for with the profits from Marich Pass curio shop.

Located in the remote West Pokot District, Marich Pass Field Studies Centre (MPFSC) is an example of working together for mutual benefit. Started by a European who has lived and worked in Kenya for over 30 years, the field centre employs around ten full-time and numerous part-time staff from the local area. The centre opens up a new area of the country to visitors and offers alternative eco-tourism attractions such as bird watching and botany tours, visits to local villages, or walks in the spectacular Cherangani Hills. Donations from visitors help fund the local school and clinic, whilst profits from the centre are used to fund projects such as irrigation and water storage or to sponsor children to complete their schooling. Local people have taken advantage of the centre, too, and set up a small curio shop selling crafts to visitors. The profits from the shop have been used to purchase a grain mill, which saves time and money for the community. The benefits of such a project are felt by the whole community and they talk proudly about the centre. They believe it has improved their lives significantly and that more such projects are needed in Kenya.

A NEW IMAGE

Perhaps the most important challenge for Kenya as it begins the twenty-first century is to present a new image to the outside world. The political violence, corruption and economic mismanagement of the 1990s have left the country with a severely dented reputation. Neighbours such as Uganda and Tanzania by contrast have entered a new stage in their development and been successful in attracting businesses and visitors that may have formerly favoured Kenya. Post-apartheid South Africa is also benefiting at Kenya's expense. Better

Tourists are increasingly being flown around Kenya to avoid its poorly maintained roads.

infrastructure and modern facilities mean South African destinations are becoming the first-choice option over Kenya for beach and safari tourists to the African continent.

But Kenya must do much more than revamp its ageing hotels and repair its worn roads if it is to regain its reputation as an ambassador for Africa. It must also address the poverty felt by the majority of its people and provide future generations with the opportunities to benefit both themselves and their country. In isolated locations such progress is visible, but massive inequalities remain.

Newspapers deliver important information, but many adults in Kenya are still illiterate.

The government must not forget the millions who cannot afford schooling or who suffer poor health due to a lack of facilities and basic medicines. It is currently focusing on boosting tourism and targeting HIV/AIDS as priorities, but unless people's basic needs are met, the country is likely to continue its roller-coaster development of the last 20 years.

BEYOND MOI

The biggest hurdle for Kenya's immediate future is to adjust to life beyond President Moi. Having been in power since 1978, Moi will finally stand down from his presidency in December 2002 after nearly a quarter of a century in control. With no clear successor to President Moi, there are concerns that tensions between different ethnic groups will come to the surface during the struggle for power. Some believe this is best resolved by turning Kenya into a federal state with each region (and ethnic group) taking more direct control of its own affairs. Others point out that if problems relating to land rights and corruption were overcome, then many of the tensions would disappear and there would be no need to carve up the country in such a manner. Whatever happens, the transition of power from Moi to the new president will be a testing time for Kenya and one the world will be watching very closely.

A POSITIVE OUTLOOK

With seemingly so many problems, it is easy to consider Kenya's future rather bleakly, but despite their difficulties most Kenyan's remain optimistic. They have great pride in their achievements to date and are continuously looking for ways to further improve their lives. The ambition and enterprise of the *jua kali* sector or of the various self-help groups around the country are good examples of this positive outlook. Certainly Kenya has much to be positive about. Its economy is among the strongest in the region and Kenya is in a good position to benefit from the renewed East Africa Community. Long-established trade links with Europe and beyond also give Kenya an advantage in an increasingly competitive global economy. More than anything else, it is the Kenyan people who offer the greatest promise for the future. Their optimism and energy is truly inspiring and something that, if experienced, will be remembered at least as well as the beautiful landscapes and stunning wildlife that attract so many visitors to Kenya in the first place.

Despite the problems Kenya faces its people remain optimistic about their future.

GLOSSARY

Agrochemicals Chemicals such as fertilisers and pesticides.

Annual temperature range The extremes of average temperature experienced in a location over the period of a year.

Arid A term used to describe an environment with an annual rainfall that is below 250–300mm.

Biodiversity The variation (diversity) of biological life within an ecosystem.

Cash crops Crops such as tea and coffee that are grown commercially.

Chemical run-off Chemicals that are washed from land or plants by rainfall or water and pollute the environment.

Colonial A term used to describe a system whereby one country is occupied and ruled by another foreign country.

Curative healthcare Healthcare that focuses on curing illness or disease as opposed to avoiding it in the first instance.

Diurnal temperature range The extremes of average temperature experienced in a location over the period of a day.

East African Community (EAC) A trading and economic co-operation between the three main nations of East Africa – Kenya, Tanzania and Uganda.

Ecosystem The contents of an environment, including all the plants and animals that live there. This could be a garden pond, a forest or the whole earth.

Eco-tourism Tourism that is sensitive to its impact on environments and local populations.

El Niño A warming of the oceans that causes changes in regional weather patterns, normally marked by extreme events such as droughts or floods.

Erosion The removal of soil or rock by the forces of nature (wind or rain) or people (deforestation).

Escarpments A more or less continuous line of cliffs or steep slopes marking a sudden difference in landscape.

Federal state A form of government in which regions of a country take greater control of their own affairs with a reduced role for the central government.

Floriculture The growing of flowers – normally in highly controlled environments involving irrigation technology and glasshouses to control humidity and temperature.

Fluorite A mineral that is mined for its fluorescent qualities.

GDP Gross Domestic Product (GDP) is the monetary value of goods and services produced by a country in a single year.

Geothermal power The use of superheated steam from deep underground to drive turbines for generating electricity.

GNP Gross National Product (GNP) is the monetary value of goods and services produced by a country plus any earnings from overseas in a single year.

Harambee A term meaning 'pull together' in Swahili and used by Kenya's first president, Jomo Kenyatta, to encourage people to work together for the good of the country.

Herbicides Chemicals used to kill unwanted plant growth considered to be weeds.

Horticulture The growing of vegetables, fruit, herbs and flowers (floriculture), normally in a highly controlled environment.

Hydroelectric power (HEP) Electricity generated by water as it passes through turbines.

Infrastructure Networks that allow communication or help people and the economy to function such as roads, railways, electricity and phone lines.

Intercropping A system of growing several crops together in such a way that each benefits the other.

Jua kali Part of the informal economy in Kenya offering valuable trades and services.

Lapse rate the rate at which air temperature cools or warms with altitude, normally expressed as degrees centigrade (°C) per 100 or 1,000m.

Leachate A liquid formed when water enters a landfill site and carries diluted chemicals and metals with it as it passes through the rubbish.

Life expectancy The expected lifetime of a person born in any particular year – measured in years.

Mortality rate The number of people who die per 1,000 people in any given year.

Pastoralists People who depend primarily on livestock for their livelihoods.

Population momentum The continued growth of a population due to a large number of young people in the population entering reproductive age.

Preventative healthcare Healthcare that focuses on preventing illness and disease from occurring through programmes such as immunisation.

Sanitation The provision of hygienic toilet and washing conditions to prevent the spread of diseases associated with human waste.

Savannah A dryland ecosystem dominated by tropical grassland with scattered trees and bushes.

Semi-arid An environment in which annual rainfall is generally between 250–600mm.

Shanty towns Makeshift settlements close to urban centres.

Sisal A plant that is harvested for its fibre, which is used in rope making or basketry.

Sustainable development Development that meets the needs of today without compromising the ability of future generations to meet their needs.

Ugali A meal made from ground maize mixed with water and boiled into a porridge or heavy bread.

FURTHER INFORMATION

BOOKS TO READ:

NON-FICTION
Country Studies: Kenya by Heather Blades (Heinemann Library, 2000) Illustrated reference for KS3-4.

World Fact Files: East Africa by Rob Bowden and Tony Binns (Hodder Wayland, 1998) Illustrated reference for KS3.

World Focus: Kenya by David Marshall and Geoff Sayer (Heinemann Library, 1994) Illustrated reference for KS2-3.

FICTION
Out of Africa by Isak Dinesen (Penguin, 1999) A classic novel set in Kenya and made into a film of the same name.

The Flame Trees of Thika by Elspeth Huxley (Pimlico, 1998) A classic autobiography about growing up as a child in East Africa.

No Man's Land by George Monbiot (Macmillan, 1994) A critical insight to the lives of the Masai and their struggle with the wildlife conservation movement.

Weep Not Child by Ngugi wa Thiong'o (Heinemann, 1964) A classic Kenyan novel by their best-known author.

Kenya: Promised Land? by Geoff Sayer (Oxfam, 1998) Series of factual essays exploring modern issues in accessible illustrated style.

WEBSITES:

TOURISM
www.kenyatourism.org/
www.kenya-wildlife-service.org/

GENERAL INFORMATION ON KENYA
www.kenyaweb.com/
www.kenyatourism.org/
www.jambokenya.com/
www.kenya-wildlife-service.org/
www.nationaudio.com/
www.africaonline.com/site/ke/

USEFUL ADDRESSES:

Kenya Tourist Office
25 Brooks Mews
Mayfair
London
W1Y 1LF

Kenyan High Commision
45 Portland Place
London
W1N 4AS

Lions feasting on a zebra. Lions also threaten nearby cattle, bringing them into conflict with local people.

INDEX

Numbers shown in **bold** also refer to pages with maps, graphic illustrations or photographs.

A boy washes his bike in Lake Victoria.

Donkeys pull a cart laden with water.